contents

introduction

Watch the television news this evening and you are likely to see a report from a war zone, possibly in the Middle East or another well-known trouble spot. You assume that what the reporter is telling and showing you is true and that the reporter is being as objective as possible. But how do you know that what you're being shown is the truth and not propaganda? How do you know if the reporter is only telling you one side of the story, or failing to give you the full facts so that you can make your own mind up about what is going on?

Today, propaganda is everywhere. It is part of our daily lives and something many of us take for granted. Its reach is vast and its importance is considerable.

But what exactly is propaganda, and how does it work?

This book sets out to explain propaganda in all its many different aspects. It looks at what propaganda is and discusses both the key players who produce it and those (like you and me) at whom it is aimed. It shows how propaganda works, how a successful propaganda campaign can be produced, and how and why some campaigns fail. Above all, it shows how important propaganda is, and how you can detect it.

Propaganda has been part of history from the earliest times right up to the present day. It was used by the ancient Greeks and Romans, the Catholic Church, and the American revolutionaries, and has played an important role in numerous wars and battles. During the 20th century, it became as much a part of warfare as guns and tanks, and was crucial in the conduct of both world wars. Under the Nazi Party in Germany, propaganda reached new levels of sophistication and ingenuity, with terrible results. During the Cold War, fought between capitalist West and communist East after 1945, propaganda was the main weapon used by both sides, for this was a war of ideas as much as of military might.

INFLUENCE AND
PERSUASION

PROPAGANDA IN WAR & PEACE

SIMON ADAMS

www.heinemann.co.uk/library
Visit our website to find out more information about **Heinemann Library** books.

To order:
☎ Phone 44 (0) 1865 888066
📄 Send a fax to 44 (0) 1865 314091
💻 Visit the Heinemann bookshop at www.heinemann.co.uk/library to browse our catalogue and order online.

First published in Great Britain by Heinemann Library, Halley Court, Jordan Hill, Oxford OX2 8EJ, part of Harcourt Education.

Heinemann is a registered trademark of Harcourt Education Ltd.

Created, designed and produced for Heinemann Library by Trocadero Publishing, An Electra Media Group Enterprise, Suite 204, 74 Pitt Street, Sydney, Australia

Originated by Modern Age
Printed in China
by WKT

ISBN 0 431 09836 0
10 09 08 07 06
10 9 8 7 6 5 4 3 2 1

British Library Cataloguing in Publication Data
Adams, Simon
Influence and Persuasion: Propaganda in War and Peace – Manipulating the Truth
303.3'75
A full catalogue record for this book is available from the British Library.

Picture credits
Associated Press 46; Brand X Pictures 5, 18, 19, 45, 47; Comstock Images 54, 55; Corbis/Sygma 12 (bottom); Electra Collection 12 (top), 14, 17, 24, 25, 26, 30, 32, 35, 36, 37, 38, 39, 44, 56, 59; Flat Earth Picture Gallery 10, 27; Kobal Collection/MGM 41; Lonely Planet Images/ Martin Moos 11; Lonely Planet Images/Jane Sweeney 13; Newspix/Leon Mead 7; Newspix 52, 58 (top); Newspix/ Robert McKell 58 (bottom); Oronsay Imagery 9, 43; Oronsay Imagery/Scott Brodie 20, 23; Popperfoto 8, 21, 28, 47 (top); Topham Picturepoint cover; US Army 48, 53; US National Archives 25, 33, 42, 43, 50, 55

Every effort has been made to contact copyright holders of any material reproduced in this book. Any omissions will be rectified in subsequent printings if notice is given to the publishers.

Disclaimer
Any Internet addresses (URLs) given in this book were correct at the time of printing. However, due to the dynamic nature of the Internet, some addresses may have changed, or sites may have ceased to exist since publication. While the author and publisher regret any inconvenience this may cause readers, no responsibility for any such changes can be accepted by either the author or the publisher.

Today, the nature of propaganda has changed. Twenty-four-hour cable television and the Internet have totally transformed the flow of news and information around the world. But as the world has changed beyond all recognition in recent years, so too has propaganda. Yet despite these many changes, propaganda will continue to play a major role in all our lives, as it has done in the past.

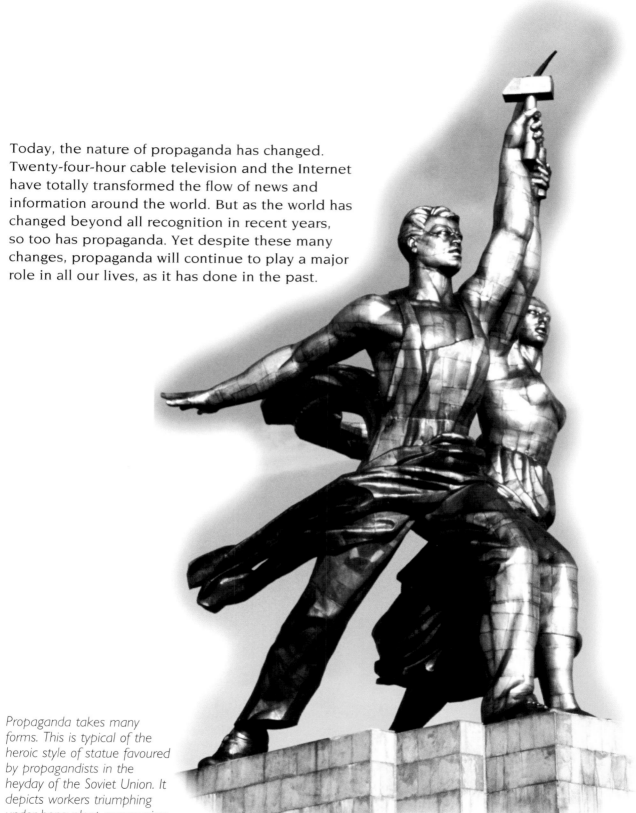

Propaganda takes many forms. This is typical of the heroic style of statue favoured by propagandists in the heyday of the Soviet Union. It depicts workers triumphing under benevolent communism.

what is propaganda?

Propaganda is the organized distribution of information or a particular set of ideas. It is a deliberate attempt to persuade people to think or act in a particular way. In the words of Garth Jowett and Victoria O'Donnell, in their book *Propaganda and Persuasion*: "Propaganda is the deliberate, systematic attempt to shape perceptions, manipulate cognitions [thoughts], and direct behaviour to achieve a response that furthers the desired intent of the propagandist."

Propaganda is a deliberate act, not just something that happens accidentally. It is also systematic, in that it is carried out in a methodical, planned way. Its goal is to attempt to shape or change people's thoughts and views about the world, or make them change their behaviour so that they act in a different way. The person carrying out the propaganda is known as the propagandist, and all this is done to further their desired intent or wishes.

Propaganda is therefore one-sided. It is intended to benefit the person or organization conducting the propaganda, not its recipient. That is why propaganda is different from information and education, both of which seek to transmit facts openly to the benefit of the recipient. It is also different from persuasion. If I try to persuade you that it is in your best interests to read a specific book, or go and watch a particular film, what I am doing is very clear and is of obvious benefit to you, and quite possibly me as well, since we can then discuss the book or film together. If you don't think there is any benefit in reading that book or watching that film, you won't do it. Persuasion is clear and open. Propaganda is usually hidden – the source of the information is concealed – and only benefits one side.

DEFINING PROPAGANDA

Propaganda:
information, especially of a biased or misleading nature, used to promote a political cause or point of view.

Source: *Concise Oxford English Dictionary*

The Olympic Games is regarded by governments around the world as a great propaganda vehicle to promote their countries.

But why would anyone want to do this? Why bother to change the way people think and act? Imagine you are a government official and you are about to start a war that you know most people disagree with. The skilful use of propaganda might persuade people that this war is a good war, and that it is worth fighting. So instead of demonstrating on the streets against the war, people might decide to join the army, or support the government in other ways.

Imagine too that you are the leader of a government running a country that has just been defeated in a terrible war. No one wants to fight any more, but you want to start another war in order to avenge your country's defeat in the first. Skilful use of propaganda might persuade people that despite that defeat, it

is worth fighting once again. If this sounds far-fetched, it is exactly what the Nazis did in Germany fifteen years after that country's defeat in World War I. The Nazis were the most skilful propagandists in history.

Types of propaganda

There are many different ways of classifying propaganda, because propaganda itself can take many different approaches. It can attempt to change people's views by stirring them up (making them active), or it can change their views by lulling them into acceptance (making them passive). One good way of understanding this complex phenomenon is by looking at the source of a particular piece of propaganda and its accuracy.

White *propaganda* comes from an obvious source whose information is largely accurate, such as a radio or television station in your home country that broadcasts a report of an international sporting event, highlighting your country's successes while ignoring the success of others. The intention here is that you feel better about your country because you know it is winning, a result achieved by not telling you how the other competitors are doing.

Black propaganda is the direct opposite of this, as the source is hidden and the information largely false. Black propaganda often occurs in wartime, such as the New English Broadcasting Station that in 1940 broadcast war news, along with the British national anthem and other patriotic songs, to British listeners.

In fact the station was German and broadcast false information in an attempt to lower British morale during the early years of World War II. Black propaganda thrives on lies, and the bigger the lies the more effective it is.

Grey propaganda comes somewhere in between the two, as the source might or might not be correctly identified, and the information might or might not be true. This makes it much harder to identify.

Religious origins

Although propaganda has been around for thousands of years, the word itself appeared for the first time in the 17th century. On 31 October 1517 the German theologian Martin Luther protested against the sale of indulgences (promises of God's forgiveness) by the Catholic Church by nailing a list of 95 theses (arguments) to the door of All Saint's Church in Wittenberg. His action was to split the church and, in a series of events now known as the Reformation, led to the creation of Protestant churches throughout Europe.

The Catholic Church countered the Protestant Reformation by reforming its own practices and stamping out dissent. In 1622 Pope Gregory XV, head of the Catholic Church, decided that his church needed a single

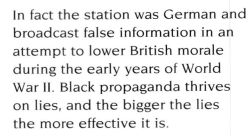

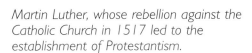

Martin Luther, whose rebellion against the Catholic Church in 1517 led to the establishment of Protestantism.

body to fight the Protestants. On 22 June he set up the Sacra Congregatio de Propaganda Fide – the Catholic Church always spoke and wrote in Latin – which in English means the Sacred Congregation for the Propagation of the Faith. This new body trained missionaries, or propagandists, to revive the faith in Protestant Europe and strengthen it in the new European colonies in the Americas.

The object of the missionaries' work was to bring people to accept the church's doctrines voluntarily. No coercion or force was to be used. The missionaries thus had to persuade people to change, often by covert or hidden ways. To do this, they attempted to control their opinions. The word "propaganda" was at first used to describe any organization that set out to spread a particular doctrine or set of beliefs, but it soon came to describe the doctrine itself, and eventually the techniques used to change opinions in order to spread that doctrine. This is the meaning of the word today.

Propaganda began as an instrument of the Catholic Church, so Protestants always viewed it in a hostile way. That negative view has continued to this day. Ask someone to come up with other words they associate

" Propaganda is a much maligned and often misunderstood word. The layman uses it to mean something inferior or even despicable. The word propaganda always has a bitter after-taste. "

Josef Goebbels, Nazi Minister for Propaganda and Public Enlightenment, March 1933

with propaganda, and they will reply with "lies", or "spin", or "mind control" – all negative words. But in fact, propaganda is neither positive nor negative, nor is it good or bad. It is just a process of manipulating someone's behaviour or views for someone else's benefit. The only way to judge propaganda is whether it is successful or not.

key players

The main aim of propaganda is to manipulate an individual's or a group's behaviour, so that they think or act in a different way. But who would want to do this, and to whom?

The biggest propagandists are institutions or organizations with a political agenda. National governments, political parties, trades unions, churches and other religious groups, pressure groups, protest movements, terrorist or subversive organizations – all these groups seek to change the world in one way or another and use propaganda in order to effect that change. So too do business organizations, multinational companies, trade organizations, professional bodies, and other groups that are involved in business and commerce. Within a government, propaganda might be conducted by the political leadership itself, or by the military or intelligence services working on their behalf.

In many cases, such organizations are up-front about their use of propaganda – the communist leaders of the Soviet Union established an organization called the Agitational-Propaganda Section of the Central Committee of the Communist Party, known as Agitprop, to deliver communist beliefs to every town and village in the country.

Both communism and Nazism used architecture as propaganda. Buildings such as this one in Poland were meant to represent the supreme power of the state.

Turkmenbashi

The most extraordinary example of personal propaganda in the world today can be seen in the central Asian republic of Turkmenistan, once part of the Soviet Union.

Since independence in 1991, the country has been ruled by President Saparmurad Niyazov, who has established a dictatorship based on a substantial personal cult. Niyazov has styled himself as the Turkmenbashi ("father of all the Turkmen") and erected statues and portraits on every street corner, square, and crossroads in the country. He has renamed the days and months of the year after his family, and his spiritual guide to life, *Ruhnama*, is compulsory reading for every student.

Underpinning this cult is the systematic use by secret police of torture and mind-altering drugs against his opponents. All public and private meetings – even weddings and funerals – must be registered with the authorities.

On public occasions, the crowd is made to chant, "Halk, Vatan, Turkmenbashi" ("One people, one empire, one leader"). In German, this translates as "Ein Volk, ein Reich, ein Führer", the slogan used by Hitler to glorify his role in Nazi Germany.

The Turkmenbashi Tower in Ashighabat. At the top is a golden statue of Turkmenbashi that revolves 360° every day, so that he always faces the sun.

We still use the word "agitprop" today to define any piece of theatre or performing art that has a political message or is viewed or promoted as being a work of political propaganda.

Adolf Hitler

Josef Stalin

The Nazi Party in Germany was even more explicit, setting up the Ministry for Propaganda and Public Enlightenment (RMVP), headed by Josef Goebbels, to spread the Nazi message throughout the country. Both the British and American governments were more covert, setting up the Ministry of Information and the Office of War Information (respectively) during World War II. However, both organizations were mainly concerned with propaganda, despite what their titles implied.

Individuals can also initiate propaganda. Both the Nazi leader Adolf Hitler and the Russian Communist leader Josef Stalin were masterful in their use of propaganda to gain and maintain power. Stalin even went to the extreme lengths of having photographs manipulated or doctored to remove the images of his enemies or those he had killed or executed as potential rivals.

Kim Jong Il, son of Kim Il Sung of North Korea, who is developing the same style of personality cult as his father.

Where once a photograph showed three or four people, later it showed just Stalin; other photographs were doctored to swell the adoring crowd at one of his speeches, or to position him more visibly or centrally in agroup photo.

In recent years, dictators such as Saddam Hussein in Iraq and Kim Il Sung in North Korea established huge personality cults in which their portraits appeared on huge posters in every town, and their every word was broadcast to the nation. The media was used to spread the message that these leaders were infallible and could do no wrong. Every possible method of propaganda was used to confirm their greatness and crush any opposition to their rule.

It is not just politicians who use propaganda to enhance their careers or status. Celebrities – for example, film stars, rock musicians, and members of the royal family – are very careful to make sure that only approved photographs of them are published and that no image appears of them looking disheveled or the worse-for-wear. Everyone likes to look their best, but celebrities have images they wish to project to their fans. Unofficial or unflattering portraits could do that image harm. Careful presentation of one's public image is usually considered to be good PR (public relations), but as such, PR is itself a form of propaganda.

One of the many murals dedicated to Saddam Hussein which were found in towns and villages across Iraq until 2003.

So who is this propaganda aimed at? The simple answer is that it is aimed at anyone who the propagandist wants to influence. The electorate or particular sections of it, such as pensioners or working mothers, are targeted by a national government or a political party, while potential believers are targeted by churches. Propaganda can be aimed at large numbers of people or a specific audience carefully chosen because of their potential receptiveness to its message.

propaganda examined

It is easy but wrong to think of propaganda as a single item or event, a one-off piece of information or misinformation that exists only for a short time. Propaganda is not so simple – it is usually produced in a coherent and often complex campaign that takes place over a period of time and has many different aspects to it. It is a flow of information, like a river, that has many different participants and draws on many different resources as it flows from its original source down to its intended audience. Because it is complex, it is necessary to analyse it in some detail to make sense of it.

One way to do this is to break propaganda down into ten separate stages. These stages can be considered as questions to ask about a propaganda campaign in order to understand it better. Let's consider them one by one. Some appear very obvious, but it is often the obvious things that are overlooked.

The ten stages

Firstly, what is the ideology behind the campaign? What is its purpose? Any propaganda campaign must have an ideology or belief behind it to give the campaign purpose. This might be a political belief – communism, for example, or free-market capitalism – or a religious belief. It might, if one is conducting a campaign on behalf of a business, be a belief in

US soldiers display a captured North Korean flag. One of the most powerful clashes of propaganda occurred with the Korean War of 1950–1953. It was characterized as a battle between western and communist ideologies, with both sides pouring out a flood of propaganda to justify their stands.

a particular product or lifestyle. It is this belief that informs a propaganda campaign and gives it direction and purpose. The Nazi propagandist Josef Goebbels said that propaganda has no single method, only purpose, which in the Nazi's case was the conquest of the hearts and minds of the Germans so that they would follow the Nazi Party and its leader Adolf Hitler without question.

Secondly, when looking at a propaganda campaign, it is important to look at the context in which it occurs. Ask questions such as what events have given rise to the campaign, what is the background to the campaign, what is the mood of both the people who are running the campaign and of those to whom it is directed, and is the campaign being conducted at a time of peace and stability, or war? Think of propaganda as a packet of seeds dropped onto fertile soil. You need to look at that soil to see how the propaganda seeds grow and spread.

The third question has already been covered in the last chapter. It is important to identify who the propagandist is. Sometimes it is very clear, but if black propaganda is used, identity is often deliberately concealed. One way to find this out is to ask who benefits or gains most from the propaganda.

Fourthly, it is also crucial to assess the structure of the propaganda organization. A successful campaign is often run by a strong decision-making authority that sends out the same message throughout the structure of the organization, from top to bottom. If an organization such as a government is weak and divided, or is acting in contradictory ways, it will send out different messages, and its propaganda will be less effective.

Fifthly, when looking at an organization such as a political party, it is helpful to distinguish between a member and a follower. Many people were Nazis or communists, but not every one of them was a member of the party. Members of a party might play an active role in a propaganda campaign, such as organizing mass rallies and demonstrations, whereas followers take a more passive role such as participating in that rally or demonstration.

1 What is the ideology and purpose of the campaign?

2 What is the context in which the campaign occurs?

3 Who is the propagandist?

4 What is the structure of the propaganda organization?

5	Who is the target audience?
6	What media techniques are being used?
7	Are there any special techniques in use to increase the effect of the campaign?
8	What is the target audience's response to the propaganda?
9	Is there any counterpropaganda?
10	How effective has the campaign been?

Some followers might be unwilling participants, who have hidden their real beliefs for fear of losing their jobs, or perhaps their lives. Followers may be the target of much of the propaganda.

We have already covered the question of who the target audience is. The sixth question to ask is, what different media techniques are used in the campaign to reach that audience? As we shall see when we examine propaganda through history, the range of media available to propagandists increased rapidly during the 20th century, as radio, television, the cinema, advertising, and other elements of mass communication were used for propaganda purposes. Today, that range is even wider, with email, fax, the Internet and the worldwide web, direct mail, and 24-hour cable and satellite television all utilized by the propagandist. These will be used in different ways according to the target audience. Looking at all the different media will help put together a complete picture of how the campaign works.

The seventh question to ask is whether any special techniques are used to increase the effect and success of the campaign. Some campaigns always use music – patriotic songs, for example, or "feel-good" music – while others may show the leading figure standing beside the national flag. One technique often employed is to work with those who have standing and status in their own community or whom the general public respects. Political parties often use film stars and musicians to endorse their programmes because of their appeal.

The eighth stage of a propaganda campaign to consider is to ask how the target audience is responding to the campaign. Opinion polls, election results, increased membership figures or financial donations, higher sales of a product or lower sales due to a boycott – all these are indicators that a campaign is hitting its mark.

The ninth stage to consider is that most propaganda campaigns will attract counter-campaigns against them. Sometimes these will take the same form as the propaganda campaign itself, but often they will adopt completely different tactics. Look to see if there is any counterpropaganda, and what form it takes, for that will give you a good idea as to how effective the initial propaganda has been. The success of Arthur Miller's counterpropaganda play *The Crucible* showed how effective the anti-communist propaganda of Senator McCarthy had been.

The final question to ask is whether the purpose of the propaganda has been fulfilled. How effective has the campaign been, has it succeeded in its main aims, and could it be repeated again? These questions are often difficult to answer, as a good propagandist will always want you to believe in the success of the campaign. It is also difficult to make a quick judgment, as the results of some campaigns might not be evident for years. After examining these ten stages, you should have a good overview of how propaganda works.

Counter-propaganda play

In the early 1950s, Senator Joseph McCarthy ran a "red scare" campaign in the USA against supposed communist infiltration of government, the armed services, and other institutions. One of the most successful pieces of counterpropaganda to this campaign was a play – *The Crucible* – by Arthur Miller, which was supposedly about trials for witchcraft in 17th-century New England. In reality, however, the play was about the dangers caused by the mass hysteria that accompanies any witch-hunt, whether of real witches or supposed communists.

history of propaganda

W̲e do not know when propaganda was first used, or by whom, but we do know that it has been in use for the whole of human history, since the time when humans first started writing around 5000 years ago.

Propaganda in ancient times

T̲he Sumerians built a flourishing civilization in Mesopotamia (the area that now includes parts of Syria, Turkey, and Iraq) around 3000 BC and kept detailed records on clay tablets using a form of picture writing known as cuneiform. Although the tablets consist mainly of trading records, they do include signs for "courier" and "herald",

Pillars of propaganda

The Sumerians erected stone pillars, or *stelae*, by their city gates or on the borders, depicting the king with his god or a beaten enemy.

On one such *stela* at Lagash, Nin-girsu, god of Lagash, is shown capturing his enemies in a net while he rides in a war chariot. On the other side, King Eannatum (reigning in around 2550 BC) is shown advancing with his army and crushing the enemy underfoot while lions and vultures devour the enemy dead.

The propaganda message of the *stela* is clear: "We, the people of Lagash, have god on our side and will crush all opposition to our rule. Surrender now while you have the chance!"

suggesting not only that messages were carried throughout the country but also that the people were kept informed of important events by heralds shouting out news in a street or other public place. Such news announcements would be authorized by the king – an early example of public propaganda on behalf of the state.

The Sumerians also erected stone pillars to intimidate their enemies, and composed epic poems celebrating their success in battle. Scenes from these poems were painted on the palace walls – an early example of celebratory propaganda designed to praise the king and keep his own subjects in line. Other civilizations in Mesopotamia and Egypt used similar techniques of state propaganda, but such propaganda was sporadic and lacked any overall coherence.

The first people to systematically apply propaganda in both war and peace were the ancient Greeks. From 800 BC, the Greeks developed a number of self-contained, powerful city-states – the best known are Athens and Sparta. These states often fought each other for control of Greece and its valuable trade in the region, using buildings and sculptures as physical propaganda to glorify their own cities at the expense of others. The Greek historian Plutarch (writing around AD 46 to 120) records how Pericles, ruler of Athens from 460 to 429 BC, "wooed the masses" by diverting money

Carvings on the face of the tomb of Rameses II are an example of celebratory propaganda. They depict the life and reign of the pharaoh in the best possible light.

designed to be used to defend the city against the Persians to fund work on the Acropolis. This was the dominant stone citadel in the middle of the city on which the Parthenon and other temples stand, and which symbolized Athenian

The Roman Empire used architecture as a form of propaganda, to inform its citizens and conquered peoples of the grandeur and power of the state. The Forum in Rome is typical of such propaganda.

power and cultural superiority. The Spartans used military poetry to encourage their armies to fight harder; other city-states erected monumental sculptures to commemorate victories over their enemies.

The Greeks also gave us the first example of deliberate disinformation. From 490 BC the Persians, led by Darius and then Xerxes, threatened to invade Greece. In 480 BC, Xerxes captured and almost destroyed

Athens. However, the Athenian navy survived, thanks to the cunning of its naval commander, Themistocles. He arranged to have messages sent to Xerxes suggesting that the many Greeks fighting in the Persian army could not be trusted, as a result of which Xerxes chose not to deploy them. He then told Xerxes that many of the Greeks in the fleet at Salamis were also planning to flee, so Xerxes sent some of his own fleet to trap them.

Themistocles then lured Xerxes's depleted fleet and army into battle at Salamis, which the Greeks won, thus saving their homeland from complete Persian domination. After a further Persian defeat the following year, Xerxes withdrew from Greece. Themistocles's disinformation plan worked, because it was based on the fact that troop defections were common at the time, so Xerxes had no reason to disbelieve the information he was receiving.

Two of the greatest generals in history – Alexander the Great and Julius Caesar – were also master propagandists. Alexander (356–323 BC) made sure that his face appeared on coins, buildings, and monuments throughout his vast empire so that everyone knew who was in charge. His marriage to a Persian princess was a symbolic way of showing that all the different peoples in his empire were equal, thus keeping them united in a way military force never could.

Alexander the Great, who inisted his image appear on coins, buildings and monuments.

people with their leaders and unite them behind their leader.

Visual symbols were also important in the spread of new religions. The early Christians used the signs of a fish and later the cross – a reminder of Christ's crucifixion – and decorated their churches with portraits of Christ and the apostles and scenes from the Bible, as few adherents could read the Bible for themselves. Muslims used the crescent, symbolizing the waxing moon and associated with special acts of devotion to Allah. In both cases, the symbols act as visual propaganda for the religion and help to spread its message.

Julius Caesar (c.100–44 BC) was even more adept. He was one of the first Romans to have his face stamped on coins during his own lifetime, rather than posthumously, and used these coins to pay his troops, reminding them who their master was. He also held triumphal processions – up to four a month at one point – and other spectacles to impress his great power and military success on the Roman population.

Later Roman emperors followed Caesar's example, as did Napoleon and Hitler much later. They all understood the importance of symbols and events to identify the

Julius Caesar was a master at propaganda, promoting his image and his power at every opportunity.

Propaganda in the early modern world

Until the 16th century, propaganda largely relied on visual symbols, such as coins or statues, as few people could read and even fewer had access to books or other written material. This changed with the development of the printing press and the use of moveable type by Johannes Gutenberg in 1450. The printing press allowed the mass-production of books, pamphlets and, for those who could not read, cartoons and other prints. It also was soon followed by the Reformation and the establishment of Protestant churches following Martin Luther's protest in 1517.

Luther (1483–1546), a German theologian, used a variety of propaganda techniques to bring about mass change in religious and social attitudes throughout Europe. His initial protest was to nail a list of 95 theses (arguments) against the Catholic Church onto a church door at Wittenberg in 1517.

The crescent is a symbol recognized by Muslims around the world.

This public gesture soon received widespread publicity when the list was printed and circulated throughout Germany. Over the next three years, 300,000 copies of his 30 letters, pamphlets and other publications were printed, quickly reaching a mass audience. Almost everything Luther wrote was directed at a particular audience and designed to win him support. All his words were quickly printed and distributed, ensuring that a mass audience was influenced by his teachings.

The fish

Early Christians used the figure of the fish not just because it was easy to draw but also because *Ichthus*, the Greek word for "fish", was an acronym in Greek for "Jesus Christ, Son of God, Saviour". It was also unclear to non-believers. At a time of persecution, such an anonymous symbol helped believers avoid unwanted attention.

Martin Luther was outraged by the Pope's financing of the construction of St Peter's Basilica in Rome (above). Wealthy business people were sold "indulgences", documents which claimed to forgive their sins and guarantee them entry into the Kingdom of Heaven after death. As Luther's action began to split Christianity, the Catholic Church countered him with a barrage of propaganda designed to bring its rebels into line.

As we have already seen, the Catholic Church responded to the Reformation by setting up the organization from which we get the word *propaganda*. By the 17th century, propaganda techniques were a normal part of the strategies used by those seeking to control or manipulate the thoughts of others. All major conflicts, notably the Thirty Years' War (1618–1648) in Europe and the Wars of the Three Kingdoms in Britain (1639–1651), were awash in leaflets, pamphlets, line drawings, posters, and other propaganda material produced by one side or the other.

Propaganda in the 18th and 19th centuries

Propaganda truly came of age during the two great revolutions of the late 18th century – the American Revolution, or war of independence against British rule, and the French Revolution. The American Revolution began in 1775 but its roots lay in earlier discontent by the American colonists at British misrule from London. The colonists were highly literate and very well informed about politics, reading a wide range of newspapers and political journals.

The main propaganda weapon of the period was the cartoon – in May 1754 Benjamin Franklin drew a cartoon of a snake cut into pieces, each one representing one of the colonies. The message to his fellow Americans was clear: "Unite or Die". This was the first cartoon ever to appear in an American newspaper, and was much ridiculed by the British. But after the British commander General Cornwallis surrendered to the victorious colonists at Yorktown in 1781, the famous pro-revolution British cartoonist James Gillray drew a

Events from the early days of the American Revolution such as the Boston Massacre, were well used by propagandists.

Master of propaganda

The Massachusetts politician Samuel Adams (1722–1803) is generally considered to be the chief propagandist of the American Revolution. He based his plans on five objectives: the aims of the revolution must be justified; the advantages of victory must be clear; the people must be roused into action by creating a hatred of the British; pro-British arguments need to be neutralized; and everything must be stated clearly so that even "the common labourer" can understand.

Adams was totally unscrupulous and used every possible propaganda method to further the colonists' cause. In 1772 he set up the Committee of Correspondence to organize propaganda for the revolution. His agents went to every political meeting and event to collect information, which was then spread by the Committee to the appropriate people for publication or distribution.

His most audacious propaganda coup was to organize the dumping of tea into Boston harbour in 1773 in protest against the British tax on tea. The event came to be known as the Boston Tea Party, and became a major piece of anti-British propaganda when the British retaliated, as Adams knew they would, by closing the harbour and sending more troops to the city.

cartoon that showed the British army totally surrounded by the now united American snake.

Many of the events of the revolution were actually rather minor affairs, but incidents such as Paul Revere's night-time horse ride to Lexington and Concord on 19 April 1775 to warn the US colonists that the British army was coming, and the early skirmishes at Lexington and elsewhere were turned by propagandists into events of major significance that have become part of America's history and mythology.

Many of the events of the French Revolution were also manipulated through skilful propaganda. The revolution is usually dated from the

The Boston Tea Party provided material for anti-British propaganda.

storming of the hated Bastille prison in Paris on 14 July 1789, the liberation of its prisoners, and its complete demolition. In fact, the prison only held seven prisoners and its demolition, which began two days after the event, was still incomplete three years later. Its liberation and destruction were, however, powerful propaganda symbols for the revolutionaries.

The paintings of Jacques Louis David (1748–1825), whose heroic depictions of the emperor Napoleon on horseback and in battle, also served as propaganda, doing much to enhance Napoleon's dominance and majesty, despite his small stature and unattractive face.

Even Napoleon's coronation as emperor in Notre Dame Cathedral in Paris was a propaganda event. A story went around that when Pope Pius VII prepared to crown him, Napoleon seized the imperial crown and placed it on his own head, symbolizing that he owed allegiance to no one but himself. Once again, David captured the image, which was then reproduced in thousands of prints for mass circulation.

Benjamin Franklin's snake cartoon was a propaganda message that reached a wide audience through an American newspaper.

propaganda in a new age

The birth of modern propaganda can accurately be dated to 1895–1896. In December 1895 the Lumière brothers gave the first commercial screening by cinematograph of a moving picture in Paris. The following May, Alfred Harmsworth (later Viscount Northcliffe) launched the *Daily Mail*, the world's first mass-circulation popular newspaper in London. In September, Guglielmo Marconi gave public demonstrations of wireless telegraphy, sending radio signals over Salisbury Plain and the Bristol Channel in England. The three components of mass communication – film, press, and radio broadcasting – were now in place.

Cinema projectionists in the early days of the movies. At the time, few people would have realized what a powerful propaganda tool this medium would become.

The growing importance of newspapers

During the 19th century, a communications revolution took place alongside the better-known Industrial Revolution. The development of faster printing presses capable of handling large print runs began in 1811 with Koenig's mechanical steam press, which could produce 1,000 copies in an hour. This rate rose to 10,000 in some 30 years later when the type was fixed to a cylinder rather than placed on a flat bed.

The growth of railways in the 1830s, the development of photography during the 1840s, and the introduction of electricity in the 1880s all allowed the press to flourish. Newspapers also became cheaper – in Britain, stamp duty on each copy sold was reduced from 4 pence to 1 penny in 1836 and then abolished in 1855. Above all, the extension of the franchise (the right to vote) to more adults and a steady rise in literacy rates created a mass readership hungry for news and opinion.

The Gettysburg Address

Not every effective piece of propaganda is recognized as such at the time. One famous example is the Gettysburg address, delivered by President Abraham Lincoln at the dedication on 19 November 1863 of a cemetery for those killed in one of the bloodiest battles of the American Civil War. The president spoke only 272 words in a speech that lasted barely three minutes, remembering those who died and pledging that their deaths were not in vain.

Some newspapers were complimentary but others were highly critical, one merely reporting that, "the president also spoke", while the *Chicago Times* called the speech "silly, flat, and dishwatery". Part of the problem was that American newspapers were not reporting the war properly and were often highly partisan – the editor of the *Chicago Times* told his staff to "telegraph fully all the news you can and when there is no news send rumours".

It thus took some time for the full significance of the address to sink in, and for the speech to assume its place as one of the finest declarations of freedom and equality ever delivered. As propaganda, its main impact was felt not in the Civil War but as a patriotic rallying cry in both the first and second world wars.

In England and Wales, the number of newspapers and periodicals published rose from 78 in 1781 to 563 in 1851, while the founding of the *New York Sun* in 1833 started the era of the popular "penny press". Similar mass-market papers soon appeared in many other countries.

As a result of this massive change, the main organ of the propagandist became the daily or weekly newspaper. Newspapers increased their newsgathering operations and increasingly used foreign correspondents to report on wars and other events overseas, as opposed to relying on official reports. This development led directly to the introduction of military censorship.

When William Russell of *The Times* covered the Crimean War of 1853–1856, he was so critical of the British army that the military authorities accused him of providing valuable information to the Russian enemy, as his dispatches could be relayed back to London and then sent on to St Petersburg by Russian agents almost before the battle had begun. As a result, in 1856 the British army issued a general order that forbade the publication of information that might help the enemy and allowed the expulsion of journalists. Now that war was the subject of daily newspaper reports, governments began to take official propaganda and censorship far more seriously.

A heroic image of British light cavalry attacking Russian positions during the Battle of Balaklava, during the Crimean War.

Propaganda in World War I

The three components of mass communication – film, press, and radio broadcasting – were to play a crucial role in the total wars of the 20th century. Although wars had always been brutal affairs, they had mainly been waged by armies on faraway battlefields, leaving civilian populations at home largely untouched. The development of the machine gun, airplane, submarine, tank, and long-range artillery changed all that. Aerial bombardment and submarine naval blockades brought war into people's homes, while mass killing on the frontline required a steady stream of recruits and conscripts to keep the armies up to strength.

War now became a national battle of wills involving every member of the population. The entire military, civilian, economic, industrial, and psychological resources of a nation were required to defeat the enemy and to avoid defeat itself. Women played as important a role as men for the first time. Keeping up morale on the home front became as important as military morale on the battlefield. Such total warfare required a new, professional approach to propaganda.

When World War I broke out in Europe in August 1914, the British won the first round of the propaganda war. Within hours of war being declared, the British cable

Atrocity propaganda

Running through the British propaganda campaign during World War I was the constant theme of German atrocities committed against women and children. In British newspaper reports, cartoons, and propaganda material, the Germans were always depicted as "brutish Huns" (although the Huns were actually from central Asia), while the French called the Germans "the Boche". This association of Germans with brutality enabled atrocity stories to stick in the public mind.

When reports of German brutality in Belgium in the early months of the war began to circulate, the British government set up a commission to examine the issue. It reported in early 1915, finding "a compelling mass of evidence" to support the claims. The report was translated into 30 languages and widely read in the USA, where it appeared five days after the sinking of the *Lusitania*, to great propaganda effect. Most historians now believe that the evidence given by Belgian refugees to the commission was false.

The German reputation for brutality was increased by the execution in October 1915 of Edith Cavell, a British Red Cross nurse working in Brussels, Belgium. She was found guilty by court martial of helping British and French soldiers to escape to neutral Holland, a charge she accepted. British propagandists used her death to give credibility to other supposed atrocities. The Germans, however, failed to use the executions of German women spies in France to counter.

One of the most effective atrocity stories was also the most false. On 10 April 1917 a German newspaper carried a report that a factory was being used to convert kadavers (corpses) into commodities such as soap. British propagandists picked up on the story but changed it so that the German government was accused of using human bodies, providing a mass of evidence to back up this new angle. In fact, the German word *kadaver* means horseflesh, as anyone with a German dictionary could have found out. But why let the truth get in the way of good propaganda!

ship *Telconia* cut the direct undersea cable linking Germany with the USA. Britain thus gained a huge advantage in the crucial propaganda battle of winning over neutral America to the Allied (British and French) side. All the news from Europe to America now had to be directed through British cables and could be censored by the British.

The British also had the advantage that Germany had started the war by invading neutral Belgium in order to attack France: "Poor Little Belgium" was an Allied rallying cry throughout the war. In addition, the Germans were very bad both at producing their own propaganda and at countering the British efforts, and made several terrible mistakes. As the German general Ludendorff remarked: "We were hypnotized by the enemy propaganda as a rabbit is by a snake. "

In order to win over the Americans, a secret war propaganda office was set up in London under the control of Charles Masterman to produce news, pamphlets, cartoons, and other material about the war that showed Britain and its allies in the best light possible. To achieve this, the British relied on persuasion rather than direct appeals, and used sympathetic Americans to present their case. An official British document stated, "It is better to influence those who can influence others than attempt a direct appeal to the mass of the population." The office had two major coups, both of them the result of German mistakes.

The Cunard liner RMS Lusitania, *which operated fast voyages between Britain and the USA. It was torpedoed off Ireland on 7 May 1915.*

On 7 May 1915 a German submarine sank the *Lusitania* passenger liner with the loss of 1,198 lives, 128 of whom were American. The American public was outraged, especially when a year later a German bronze medal was produced commemorating the event. In fact, the medal was created as a limited edition on the private initiative of its artist, Goetz, in order to justify the submarine campaign to the German people. The British quickly obtained one of the medals and placed a photograph of it in the *New York Tribune*. The British then faked thousands of medals in presentation boxes, each with a full "explanatory" leaflet, and distributed them widely, creating a hugely successful propaganda coup.

British promotional material for the faked German medal "commemorating" the sinking of the Lusitania.

Please do not destroy this

When you have read it carefully through kindly pass it on to a friend.

A German Naval Victory

"With joyful pride we contemplate this latest deed of our navy. . . ."—
Kölnische Volkszeitung, 10th May, 1915.

This medal has been struck in Germany with the object of keeping alive in German hearts the recollection of the glorious achievement of the German Navy in deliberately destroying an unarmed passenger ship, together with 1,198 non-combatants, men, women and children.

On the obverse, under the legend "No contraband" (*Keine Bannware*), there is a representation of the *Lusitania* sinking. The designer has put in guns and aeroplanes, which (as was certified by United States Government officials after inspection) the *Lusitania* did *not* carry, but has conveniently omitted to put in the women and children, which the world knows she *did* carry.

On the reverse, under the legend "Business above all" (*Geschäft über alles*), the figure of Death sits at the booking office of the Cunard Line and gives out tickets to passengers, who refuse to attend to the warning against submarines given by a German. This picture seeks apparently to propound the theory that if a murderer warns his victim of his intention, the guilt of the crime will rest with the victim, not with the murderer.

Replicas of the medal are issued by the Lusitania Souvenir Medal Committee, 32, Duke Street, Manchester Square W. 1.

All profits accruing to this Committee will be handed to St. Dunstan's Blinded Soldiers and Sailors Hostel.

Even more successful was the use of the Zimmermann telegram in early 1917. The British had broken all three German naval codes in the early months of the war and soon obtained all their diplomatic codes. Armed with this information, they could read virtually all German coded cable messages. On 16 January 1917 the night duty officers in room 40 of the Admiralty Office in London intercepted and deciphered a telegram from the German foreign minister, Arthur Zimmermann, to the German ambassador to Mexico. In it he proposed that unrestricted submarine warfare should start against all enemy and non-combatant shipping supplying the Allies, including American ships, and suggested an alliance with Mexico should the USA enter the war against Germany. The British handed a copy to the Americans, who published it on 1 March. One month later, on 6 April 1917, the USA entered the war on the Allied side. The British had won the propaganda battle against the Germans. The French, too, had their own propaganda successes.

A week after entering the war, the US government set up its own propaganda organization, the Committee on Public Information (CPI), run by the journalist George

US soldiers, known as "doughboys", disembark from the liner Leviathan *after their arrival in France in 1917, during World War I.*

Creel. Its aim was to tell Americans why they were involved in a war being fought more than 4,000 miles away in another continent when their own homeland was – apart from the submarine threat to shipping – not directly threatened. A network of speakers known as the Four Minute Men toured the country, giving four-minute snapshot speeches about the war – while Hollywood film stars such as Charlie Chaplin and Douglas Fairbanks starred in propaganda films produced by the War Cooperation Committee of the Motion Picture Industry.

The CPI also produced its own propaganda films, including a weekly newsreel, and designated the US Army Signal Corps as the official film unit. With 80 million Americans watching a movie every week, the power of the cinema to inform and persuade was massive.

Patriotic propaganda from the US government during World War I.

propaganda & total warfare

World War I ended on 11 November 1918 when Germany, worn out by the fighting, short of munitions and other supplies, and faced with rebellions and mutinies at home, agreed an armistice (ceasefire) with the Allies. The following year it was forced to accept humiliating peace terms at Versailles in France; if it failed to accept the terms, the Allies would start the war again. But while Germany had been forced to agree the peace terms, it had not in fact been defeated on the battlefield, nor had any of its territory been invaded, nor had it surrendered. Very soon, the myth arose in Germany that war was lost because it had been betrayed by communists, liberals, Jews, and other agitators at home, while its soldiers had lost the will to fight because of effective allied propaganda. Germany had been "stabbed in the back".

The rise of the Nazis

One German soldier wrote, "In 1915 the enemy started his propaganda among our soldiers. From 1916 it steadily became more intensive and at the beginning of 1918, it had swollen into a storm cloud. One could now see the effects of this gradual seduction. Our soldiers learned to think the way the enemy wanted them to think." The author was Adolf Hitler writing in *Mein Kampf* ("My Struggle"), the book in which he outlined his political ideas.

Hitler on propaganda

"Germany had failed to recognize propaganda as a weapon of the first order whereas the British had employed it with great skill and ingenious deliberation. ...

An effective propaganda must be limited to very few points and must harp on this in slogans ... As soon as you sacrifice this slogan and try to be many-sided, the effect will drain away."

Adolf Hitler in *Mein Kampf*, talking about Germany's failure in World War I

Adolf Hitler had been a soldier in World War I, but in 1919 he joined a small right-wing political group in Munich that soon became the National Socialist German Workers' Party, or the Nazis. In 1923 he led an abortive coup in Munich against the German state government of Bavaria, hoping to seize power and then march on Berlin to take over the country.

While in prison for his part in the Munich uprising, he wrote *Mein Kampf*. In it, he devoted two chapters to propaganda: "Its task is not to make an objective study of the truth", he wrote. "Its task is to serve our right, always and unflinchingly." He laid down five rules for successful propaganda: avoid abstract ideas and appeal instead to human emotions; employ constant repetition of a few simple ideas; put forward only one side of the argument; constantly criticize enemies of the state; and concentrate on one enemy for special vilification (in Hitler's case, he chose the Jews).

Throughout the Nazi rise to power in 1933 and during the twelve years of the Third Reich government and World War II, Hitler and his chief propagandist, Josef Goebbels, stuck to these basic rules. Goebbels also added another myth to the one of German betrayal: that of Hitler's own genius and willpower that could overcome all obstacles to make Germany great again. They found fertile ground for their message of German supremacy, racial purity, anti-Semitism, and anti-communism.

Josef Goebbels

Josef Goebbels (1897–1945) was born at Rheydt, western Germany and received his doctorate of philosophy from Heidelberg University in the 1920s. A bad limp prevented him fighting in World War I.

Disillusioned with post-war Germany, he joined the Nazi Party, taking charge of the Nazi propaganda machine. In 1933, when the party took power, he became Reich Minister for Propaganda and Public Enlightenment.

His cynical understanding of psychology made him a brilliant propagandist. He expertly used radio and cinema to advance the Nazi cause.

This image used for the 1936 Berlin Olympics emphasized the Nazi philosophy of promoting a superior Aryan people.

The Nazis used every propaganda weapon possible, first to win power, and then to enlist total support from the German people for their rule. Their main propaganda technique was the power of Hitler's and Goebbels's oratory, which used emotional language to whip up an audience to fever pitch. To make sure everyone heard the Nazi message, the new government produced a cheap, one-channel radio set – the Volksempfänger – for the masses and made it compulsory for radios with loudspeakers to be installed in factories, restaurants, and public places. Posters and other visual means, notably the cinema, were used rather than newspapers, for the emotional appeal of Nazism did not easily translate into the written word.

The Nazis were very keen on symbols, using the swastika, the eagle, the Heil Hitler salute, and even the design of buildings to emphasize their power and authority. Huge public rallies staged at Nuremberg employed these symbols to great effect. Each event was carefully choreographed with floodlights, thousands of people waving banners and flags, crowd-pleasing speeches, and stirring music. The finale of each rally was Hitler standing alone on a podium, speaking to the German people. Even a supposedly international event, the Olympic Games (held in Berlin in 1936), was stage-managed to glorify Nazi achievements.

The Nazis achieved huge success in their propaganda campaigns because theirs was the only message Germans received. All opposition was crushed, while the simple but effective Nazi slogans and messages were repeated again and again to achieve total, blind obedience from the German people. After World War II began in 1939, newsreels became increasingly important, bringing news of military successes first in western Europe and then, after the invasion of Russia in June 1941, in the east. These newsreels were not informative but were designed to give an emotional impression of

German military might through visuals and sound. Anti-British feature films were produced, while posters, cartoons, and newspaper articles made fun of Winston Churchill (the British prime minister), and the royal family. When the tide of war turned against Germany in 1943, Goebbels achieved even greater success by stiffening German morale against Allied calls for unconditional surrender. He hammered home the theme of "no capitulation" with the slogan "Hard times, hard work, hard hearts" and tied German patriotism and Nazi propaganda together even more closely.

Totalitarian propaganda

The Nazi Party was not the only political party to use propaganda. The Bolshevik (communist) Party in Soviet Russia and fascist parties in both Italy and Spain were also skilled at using propaganda to maintain their hold on power. In Russia, the Bolshevik Party had built up its support through propaganda newspapers such as I*skra* ("The Spark") and P*ravda* ("Truth"), often printed on underground presses or imported from abroad as the party was banned in Russia.

The Nazis' massive Nuremberg rallies were expertly stage-managed to achieve the maximum propaganda effect.

As opposition grew to Russia's involvement in World War I and the weak leadership of Tsar Nicholas II, the Bolsheviks used slogans such as "Peace, Land, and Bread" and "All Power to the Soviets" to get their revolutionary message across.

After they seized power in November 1917, setting up the world's first communist state, the Bolsheviks used propaganda to win over an often-hostile population. The main problem they faced was that about 60 per cent of Russian adults were illiterate. Most Russians were, however, very receptive to visual images, as the Russian Orthodox Church had always used icons of Christ and the saints to teach the scriptures. The Bolsheviks used

Nazi propagandists were firm believers in recruiting young children to the party's cause.

visual images such as posters and, above all, films: the Russian leader Lenin said that, "for us, the most important of all arts is the cinema". By the mid-1920s thirteen film studios were turning out well over 100 full-length propaganda films a year. The most famous of these were produced by Sergei Eisenstein: both *Battleship Potemkin* (1925) and *October* (1927) used documentary techniques to show important events in the Bolsheviks' rise to power.

The young guerrilla fighter Liu Hulan (left) was promoted as a heroine of the Chinese communist struggle in the 1940s.

In the countryside, the Bolshevik message was spread by "agit-trains", and by "agit-ships" sailing down the rivers: each of these mobile propaganda units carried about 100 party officials and was decorated with posters, red flags, and slogans. At each stop, the crowd would be entertained with films and indoctrinated with speeches, while the officials attempted to persuade local people to join the party and spread the revolution. Propaganda offices, known as "agitpunkts", were set up at local railway stations to give out information and organize local Bolsheviks. In this way, the Bolsheviks managed to get their message across to the scattered, remote rural communities where most Russians lived.

Allied propaganda

World War II saw the biggest propaganda battle ever waged in history. Even more so than the previous world war, this was a total war in which the entire population was involved and every propaganda weapon was required to boost morale and defeat the enemy. The war was also a battle between competing ideologies – between communism, Nazism, and liberal democracy – so the war of ideas was crucial.

The British approach to wartime propaganda was totally different to that of the Nazis. The Ministry of Information (MOI), set up to co-ordinate British propaganda, was run in the early part of the war by Lord Reith, former director-general of the British Broadcasting Corporation (BBC). He believed that news should be "the shocktroops of propaganda". The MOI motto became "the truth, nothing but the truth, and, as near as possible, the whole truth".

V for Victory

One of the most successful British campaigns was "V for Victory", which partly derived from Churchill's famous two-fingered victory sign.

In January 1941 the head of the BBC Belgian service suggested that the letter V should be displayed wherever possible, as it stood for the French *victoire* and the Dutch and Flemish *vrijheid* (freedom). V in Morse code was dot-dot-dot-dash, the same rhythm as the opening notes of Beethoven 's Fifth Symphony, which introduced many BBC broadcasts to occupied Europe.

The campaign was a great success in raising morale and building resistance to Nazi occupation.

V

Posters were used to lift morale – the face of Churchill appeared with the slogans "Let Us Go Forward Together" and "We're Going to See it Through" – to prevent rumours – "Careless Talk Costs Lives" – and for many other uses. The film industry was mobilized to produce patriotic films such as Laurence Olivier's *Henry V* (1944) and numerous newsreels and information films. A typical evening at the cinema would show a newsreel, an official short film, a supporting film, and the main feature, which most people had come to see. Skilfully handled propaganda inserted into this feature was the most effective, as the MOI recognized that "for the film to be good propaganda, it must also be good entertainment".

Some censorship was necessary to prevent the enemy benefiting from information broadcast, but once news reports were cleared for publication, newspapers were allowed to handle them in any way they liked. As a result, British propaganda gained the reputation for telling the truth, while the BBC acquired huge influence both at home and throughout occupied Europe for its factual reporting and for its status as a beacon of freedom and hope.

"The motion picture industry could be the most powerful instrument of propaganda in the World. whether it tries to be or not."

American president
Franklin D. Roosevelt, 1942

Teresa Wright and Greer Garson in MGM's wartime propaganda effort Mrs Miniver.

The Japanese attack on the American Pacific fleet at Pearl Harbor in December 1941 brought the USA into the war on the Allied side. Hollywood, the home of the US film industry, went to war as well, producing hundreds of morale-boosting feature films. Some of them, such as *Mrs Miniver* (1942), sympathetically portrayed Britain at war for a US audience often unaware of what its new ally had suffered in the early years of the conflict.

Well-known fictional characters such as Tarzan, Sherlock Holmes, and Batman were all enlisted for propaganda purposes, often fighting Nazi agents in far-away countries. US war films had five main purposes, as determined by the Office of War Information set up in June 1942: to explain to Americans why they were fighting; to portray the Allies and their people; to encourage work and production at home; to boost morale at home; and to depict the heroics of the armed services. Like the British, the Americans deployed truth as the main element of their propaganda. The sheer size of the US film industry – more than 80 million Americans went to the cinema each week, and the vast majority of films shown around the world were American – meant that US propaganda was widely broadcast around the world.

the cold war

In 1945 World War II ended with the total defeat of Germany and Japan and the triumph of Britain, the USA, and the USSR. But within a few years, two of the victorious wartime allies had fallen out among themselves. On the one side were the USA and other pro-western, capitalist nations; on the other, the USSR and its communist supporters. For more than 40 years, until the collapse of the USSR in 1991, these two sides fought a bitter conflict of ideology and words. This conflict was known as the Cold War, as neither side fought the other directly, although numerous wars were fought by proxies or allies of the main protagonists in Korea, Vietnam, the Middle East, Africa, central America, and Afghanistan.

Both sides depicted themselves as good and the other as evil. President Truman of the USA spelt this out in 1948: "Our way of life is based upon the will of the majority, and is distinguished by free institutions, representative government, free elections, guarantees of personal liberty, freedom of speech and religion, and freedom from political repression. The second way of life is based upon the will of a minority imposed upon the majority. It relies upon terror and repression, a controlled press and radio, fixed elections, and the suppression of personal freedoms."

All smiles for allies Winston Churchill (Britain), Franklin D. Roosevelt (USA), and Josef Stalin (USSR) at their Yalta meeting in 1945. Within a short time the USA and USSR would become opponents in what was called the Cold War.

US President Harry S Truman signs the documents authorizing the involvement in the United Nations action in Korea.

The Korean War

The first major conflict of the Cold War took place in Korea, eastern Asia, in 1950. Communist North Korea, backed by the USSR and China, invaded South Korea, backed by the USA, in an attempt to unify the peninsula under communist control. An international force organized by the United Nations but largely composed of US soldiers supported South Korea. One of the propaganda techniques used by the communists was "brainwashing", derived from the Chinese words *hse nao*, to "wash brain".

In early 1952 the communists claimed that UN forces had conducted germ warfare and caused the series of epidemics that were sweeping North Korea. Thirty-eight out of 78 captured US pilots eventually "confessed" their guilt to this charge. In fact, no such germ-warfare campaign had ever existed, but the pilots had been subjected to brainwashing by physical or mental torture to make them confess.

The USSR countered by depicting the USA as a threat to world peace, intent on establishing a new empire based on American economic domination and the suppression of communism. Both sides recognized that, in the words of one US official in the early 1960s, "the balance of power between ourselves... will be largely determined by public opinion". The way to influence public opinion was through propaganda.

The UN force's beachhead at Inchon, following General MacArthur's successful attack on North Korean forces.

Indeed, about 15 per cent of all US prisoners in North Korea had actively collaborated with the enemy as a result of brainwashing. The North Korean propaganda campaign was a brilliant success, as it portrayed the North Korean people as suffering at the hands of an evil enemy that used biological weapons against them. Only when the pilots returned home and were tried by courts of inquiry for co-operating with the enemy did the truth emerge. By then the propaganda battle was lost.

A "confession"

"The words were mine, but the thoughts were theirs. This is the hardest thing I have to explain: how can a man sit down and write something he knows is false, and yet, to sense it, to feel it, to make it seem real?"

US Marine Corps Colonel Frank Schwable, explaining his "confession" to the North Korean charge of conducting germ warfare, 1954

The role of television and radio

During the Cold War, both sides made extensive use of radio broadcasts. By 1960 Soviet radio stations broadcast 1,200 hours a week to foreign countries while Voice of America – the official international radio service of the US Information Agency (USIA) – easily matched it. The cost of this was immense: the total USIA budget in

During the Cold War radio broadcasting was a key element in the flow of propaganda from both sides.

1960 was US$100 million, while it is estimated the Soviets spent the equivalent of US$2 billion a year on all forms of propaganda.

Most propaganda radio stations broadcast white propaganda, where the source of the broadcast and its content were obvious, but a few broadcast black propaganda, where source and content were hidden. Radio Swan was financed by the American Central Intelligence Agency and broadcast black propaganda to Cuba in an attempt to destabilize and overthrow the revolutionary government of Fidel Castro. In 1985 the station was replaced by the white-propaganda service of Radio Marti, which openly broadcast from the USA "the truth, hard facts, and dispassionate analysis" about the Cuban government and its policies in the hope of breaking its monopoly of information. By 1989, according to Radio Marti's own Office of Audience Research, about 85 per cent of Cubans over 13 years old listened to the station.

> **"Our aim is propaganda, the propaganda of the party and the state. We do not hide this."**
>
> Editor-in-chief of *Pravda* ("Truth"), the Russian Communist Party's official newspaper, 1978

Fidel Castro, a prime target for US propaganda since he became president of Cuba in 1959.

after José Marti, a hero of the 1895–1898 Cuban revolution against Spain). Like the radio station, it broadcast entertainment and political messages both to break the Cuban government's total censorship of news and opinion and as a form of psychological warfare against an already beleaguered government.

Although TV Marti does not have the reach of its radio partner, it does force the Cuban government to spend a great deal of money trying to jam its signals, and shows Cubans what life outside the island is like.

Television played a less important role in most Cold War propaganda, as most television channels at the time were essentially a domestic broadcasting service with little international impact. As such, they were often used by national governments to deliver social propaganda about birth control or adult literacy to their own populations, sometimes hiding these messages within soap operas or other entertainment programmes. There are, however, three important exceptions to this rule.

The first was the role played by domestic television in the United States during the Vietnam War, an issue we will examine in the next chapter. The second is TV Marti, set up in 1990 as the television partner to Radio Marti (both were named

AIDS

One of the most successful pieces of black propaganda in recent years occurred during the early 1980s. A new illness – AIDS, which stands for Acquired Immune Deficiency Syndrome – emerged, for which there was no known cause or cure.

A rumour started that AIDS was in fact a product of an American biological warfare experiment that had gone wrong, letting the deadly virus escape and infect numerous people around the world. In fact, this story was false propaganda, circulated by Soviet secret agents. The "truth" about this lie only came out after the collapse of the USSR in 1991.

The third example is the role that television played in the ending of communism and the Cold War. The divided city of Berlin had been the focus of the Cold War ever since 1945, and at times threatened to turn the Cold War hot, notably when the communists blockaded the western half of the city in 1948–1949 and again when they built the Berlin Wall across the city in 1961.

Government propaganda in East Germany stated that the communist governments there and elsewhere in Eastern Europe were building a better society that everybody could enjoy. However, they were powerless to stop their citizens watching television broadcasts from West Germany and West Berlin, which revealed a stark contrast between the drab reality of life in the east and the increasingly prosperous lifestyles enjoyed in the west. No amount of communist propaganda could overcome television propaganda from the west.

East German soldiers guarding the Berlin Wall during its construction in 1961. Initially just rows of barbed wire, it was gradually strengthened during the 1960s.

A memorial to people who died trying to escape to the west across the Berlin Wall.

success &
failure

Propaganda is not something that is done for its own sake. It is done with intent, to persuade people to change their thoughts or views about the world and act in the way the propagandist wants them to. The ultimate aim of the propagandist is to succeed. But how do we know if a propaganda campaign has been successful, or if it has failed?

For propaganda to succeed, its intentions should be seen, understood, remembered, and acted upon. It fails when people do not act or do not respond to it. Two examples from recent history – both involving the use of American troops fighting a war abroad – show how propaganda campaigns can succeed, and fail.

A desert patrol during the Gulf War (1990–1991). This conflict was a good example of propaganda management. Media reporters' movements were strictly controlled and the stories they filed while with coalition forces were subject to many limitations.

A successful campaign: The Gulf War

In August 1990 Saddam Hussein of Iraq invaded and occupied the oil-rich neighbouring country of Kuwait. The USA led an international coalition of 29 countries to liberate Kuwait, and after a bombing campaign that started in January 1991, coalition troops expelled the Iraqis in a 100-hour land battle in February. The Iraqi propaganda campaign concentrated on the desire for Arab unity and the removal of western (US) interests in the region, while the US propaganda campaign concentrated on the right of Kuwait to enjoy freedom. In reality, the state was far from democratic.

The US-led coalition won the propaganda war by strictly controlling the media and presenting a sanitized view of the conflict. Most of the 1,500 journalists covering the war were confined to hotels in Saudi Arabia, where they received daily military press briefings, while only a few were allowed to visit the frontline. Saddam Hussein countered by allowing foreign journalists to remain in his capital, Baghdad, throughout the war and watch the coalition bombardment of the city. He hoped that television coverage of civilian casualties would turn western opinion against the war. However, the coalition highlighted its use of "smart" weapons such as guided cruise missiles to attack specific targets, rather than indiscriminate bombing. Many people watching the war on television therefore considered it more of a hi-tech video game than an actual war in which real lives might be lost.

The reality of the war was, however, very different. Only about 10 per cent of the coalition weapons were "smart"; the rest were traditional bombs dropped from planes. Many thousands of Iraqis were killed, yet the coalition propaganda campaign presented the war as a safe, clean conflict, designed to restore freedom to an oppressed nation with minimal civilian casualties. Even when a "smart" missile killed 400 Iraqi civilians in one attack, the Iraqis were unable to capitalize on it as the coalition presented it as an unfortunate accident. Many western broadcasters refused to show the pictures, which they thought would offend their viewers. As a result, support for the war around the world remained high, and Iraq failed to convince the world that its cause was right.

Formula for success

For propaganda to succeed, its intentions should be seen, understood, remembered, and acted upon.

During the Vietnam War, US planes dropped nearly 50,000 million propaganda leaflets on Vietnam, nearly 1,500 for every man, woman, and child in the country, both north and south.

In the First Gulf War of 1990–1991, US planes dropped about 29 million leaflets over Iraqi lines, 50–60 for each Iraqi soldier. Announcements made over loudspeakers to the Iraqi frontline gave instructions on how to surrender safely, while radio broadcasts encouraged desertion or surrender. In all, 60–80,000 Iraqi soldiers surrendered as a result of this propaganda campaign.

A failed campaign: The Vietnam War

If the American propaganda campaign in the Gulf War succeeded, its earlier campaign in Vietnam did not. Ever since the division of Vietnam into a communist-controlled North and a pro-western South Vietnam in 1954, communist troops had fought to reunite the country under northern control. The world's leading communist nations, the USSR and China, supported North Vietnam. The USA feared that communism might spread throughout the region and backed South Vietnam, sending increasingly large numbers of military and other advisers to the country. In August 1964 US warships came under attack from North Vietnamese gunboats in the Gulf of Tonkin. US president Lyndon Johnson used this as an excuse to send troops to support the South Vietnamese government.

In fact the entire Tonkin incident was staged by the USA to provoke North Vietnam into military action, thus providing an excuse for war. A similiar use of propaganda continued throughout the war, which ended with the US withdrawal of troops in 1973 and the eventual unification of Vietnam under communist control in 1975.

Information about the total number of US troops involved and where they were fighting (including the secret bombing of neighbouring Cambodia and Laos) was supressed, while the fatalities reported at the daily press briefings – or the "five o'clock follies", as the press described them after 1965 – were regularly distorted.

The US propaganda campaign inside Vietnam had two aims: to undermine and eventually end support for communist North Vietnam, and to win the hearts and minds of all Vietnamese – north and south – for the government of South Vietnam. Although the various campaigns had some success – more than 200,000 people came over to the South Vietnamese side or were won over to its ideology between 1963 and 1972 – its overall effect was limited. US bombing of North Vietnam created a wave of Vietnamese patriotism against American "colonialists" and "imperialists", while many just wanted the war to end so that they could live in peace.

US Marines cross a river in Vietnam at the height of the conflict in the 1960s.

Even more unsuccessful was the propaganda campaign conducted by the US government at home. At first, the traditional appeal was made to American patriotism and its obvious symbol, the flag. However, it proved difficult to convince Americans that their country was in danger when the conflict was so far away. Instead, the American public slowly became convinced through television reports that this was a conflict that the USA could not win and in which they should not be involved.

Every day, military spokespeople reported successes against a small and disorganized enemy, while television news broadcasts showed the exact opposite. In 1968 North Vietnamese troops stormed the US embassy in Saigon, capital of South Korea. As the CBS newsreader Walter Cronkite remarked: "What the hell is going on? I thought we were winning the war." From then on, television news broadcasts became more critical of the official line, while public opinion turned against the war. Television revealed that the gap between official propaganda and events on the ground was too great, and that the US propaganda campaign had failed.

From the North Vietnamese side

The communist government of North Vietnam was very adept at propaganda aimed at both its own people and people in western nations.

Its tightly controlled media delivered a never-ending barrage of stories about the actions of the USA and its allies, to convince its peoples that their fight was against neo-colonialists and imperialists trying to crush the Vietnamese spirit. These were the days before satellite television broadcasts or the Internet, when all the government had to do was block radio broadcasts from the other side.

For the rest of the world, the North Vietnamese were regularly characterized as a valiant people who had thrown off the yoke of French colonialism, only to have the US attempt to reinstate it. While the US tried to portray Vietnam as trying to spread communism to other nations, North Vietnam was able to convince much of the world it was fighting a war for freedom within its own borders.

The image of the tough North Vietnamese soldier fighting in the jungle against the odds was aided by the tremendous firepower being directed at them by the US and its allies.

Around the world, influential people began promoting the North Vietnamese cause, eroding the US military campaign even further.

future of propaganda

During the last decade of the 20th century, a new information revolution took place that was as far-reaching and important as the communications revolution of the 19th century. The development of digital technology, the rapid growth of the Internet, email, and fax, the ready availability of cheap personal computers, and the increasing range of cable and satellite networks all combined to allow information, news, and opinion to spread around the world far faster and more widely than ever before.

International news companies such as CNN produce 24-hour rolling news broadcasts that are viewed simultaneously on every continent, while digital printing technology allows the same newspapers and magazines to be printed in different cities on different continents at the same time.

At the same time as this information revolution took place, the political map of the world also changed. The Cold War came to an end in 1991 with the collapse of the USSR and the effective end of communism as a threat to the western world. President George Bush, US president from 1989 to 1993, spoke of a "new world order" in which the USA became the world's only superpower and the old conflicts between east and west would be replaced by a more collaborative order based on peace, free trade, and mutual understanding. In reality, the world

Moving images have become the major tool of propagandists today. Televisioncommands huge audiences around the world. TV news organizations prefer short, catchy images and words for their bulletins. These requirements make it ideal for disseminating propaganda.

has become more violent, with major wars occurring in Kuwait, Iraq, Afghanistan, and elsewhere.

Both these developments have had a huge impact on propaganda. For most of the Cold War (c.1947–1991), radio was the main medium for propaganda. The end of the Cold War, however, was broadcast live on television. As demonstrations and revolutions broke out across communist-run Eastern Europe in 1989, events in one country were broadcast live to the others, encouraging new protests and demonstrations.

The leaders of the Polish Solidarity movement – the first free trade union in the communist world and the main opponents of the Polish communist regime – believed that television was the most important contributor to the overthrow of communism and the establishment of democracy in the region.

The full impact of television became clear during the Gulf War of 1990–1991, when, as we have already seen, live and continuous CNN broadcasts from Baghdad did much to shape world opinion about the war and reinforce US propaganda that this was a "clean" war against specified targets in order to liberate a country, and not a war against the Iraqi people.

Destroying Saddam Hussein's propaganda images. The world has become more violent rather than more peaceful as was hoped at the end of the Cold War.

Coming of the Internet

Alongside television, the Internet is rapidly growing in importance as a means of propaganda. The Internet can provide information on almost any subject in the world, but because of its international range and easy accessibility, it is almost impossible to police or censor. It is also very difficult to find out where the information is coming from, as it is easy for a source to remain anonymous. As a result, conspiracy theories, rumours, false information, libels, and other examples of black propaganda flourish on the Internet. Such stories are often presented as fact, forcing those who are their target to deny them while confirming to others what they already believe to be true. But white propaganda also flourishes: there are numerous websites giving out information on everything from avoiding heart disease to protecting the environment.

Together, television and the Internet are increasing the amount of information that is easily available to us, and thus the amount of propaganda that we receive. In recent years, propaganda has acquired a negative meaning, but for each racist who wants to use propaganda to spread racial hatred, there are a hundred people who want to use propaganda to spread information about peace or racial harmony or safeguarding the planet. Propaganda can spread truth as well as lies, and have a positive rather than a negative impact. In the last chapter of this book we will look at what you can do to make this happen.

The past decade has seen an explosion in the use of the Internet by all levels of society and ages around the world.

The Internet

The Internet, like many recent inventions, was a product of the Cold War. In 1957 the USA set up the Advanced Research Projects Agency (ARPA) to develop new military and civilian technologies to counter the Soviet threat.

Its research was stored on individual computers housed in separate scientific research establishments, which made the project vulnerable to attack should war break out. As a result, in 1969 the US army set up the ARPAnet to link computers together via telephone lines, radio networks, and satellite links to create a safe information network.

Major US universities and research laboratories soon became involved, while the National Science Foundation (NSF) set up its own computer network linking five university supercomputers. In 1983 ARPAnet merged with the NSF network, creating the core of the Internet that we know today.

The Internet grew rapidly and was helped by the invention in 1989 of the World Wide Web, a method of Internet navigation developed by the British scientist Tim Berners-Lee.

propaganda & you

In October 1937 Professor Clyde R. Miller of Columbia University, New York City, set up the Institute for Propaganda Analysis (IPA). Miller had been a reporter during World War I and believed that he and many others had been deceived by the propaganda put out by both sides, notably the British. At the outbreak of World War II he was concerned that as the world returned to war, the USA would once again be drawn into a European conflict because of European propaganda. He was also concerned that domestic propaganda from communists, the racist Ku Klux Klan, and other groups was threatening US democracy. Because of this propaganda, Americans had, in the words of one IPA supporter, "lost their capacity to think things through".

Every month the institute published *Propaganda Analysis*. Its second issue contained the article, "How to Detect Propaganda", listing seven common devices or tools used in propaganda. These seven tools help us identify propaganda, but are also useful if you want to construct your own propaganda campaign on behalf of a person or idea, or indeed yourself. The article listed the seven as: name calling, glittering generality, transfer, testimonial, plain folk, card stacking, and bandwagon. Let's look at them one by one.

Richard Nixon (right) and his family depart the White House for the last time in 1974, following his resignation. In the aftermath a great deal of propaganda has been disseminated in an attempt to rehabilitate his image which was destroyed by the Watergate scandal.

Name calling is the simplest propaganda trick in the book. Give a person or an idea a bad name, and keep doing so repeatedly, regardless of the truth and without examining the evidence. This is also known as "smear tactics".

Glittering generality describes the practice of linking someone or something with a "virtue word" such as "honest" or "trustworthy" to make them or it acceptable, regardless of the truth and without examining the evidence. For example, if you keep saying that a political party is "new", people will believe that it is indeed a new party and not the old party it once was, and vote for it. Glittering generalities can also be negative and used to attack one's opponents.

Mahatma Gandhi led India's fight for independence from British colonial rule. His powerful appeal to all Indians led to a barrage of smear tactics being directed at him by the colonial administrators as well as those who sought to challenge his leadership of the movement.

Whatever happened to the I.P.A.?

After its launch in 1937, the Institute of Propaganda Analysis enjoyed great success. It set up an education campaign to encourage its members and journal readers to gather material so that they could analyse propaganda for themselves, and promoted critical discussion and investigation of propaganda and related issues.

Its main publication – *A Group Leader's Guide to Propaganda Analysis* – showed how analysis of propaganda could be used to understand advertising, politics, even music and art. By September 1939 its publications were used in more than 550 US schools and colleges, as well as numerous local societies, and its work was increasingly respected.

The Institute suspended operations in October 1941, when it appeared that the USA was bound to enter World War II, as it felt that its work could be used to undermine the government at a time of national emergency. By the time the war ended, the political climate in the USA had changed massively, and the IPA's techniques were no longer relevant. It never returned.

Propaganda against refugees

A great deal of propaganda is directed at refugees and asylum seekers. They are portrayed as selfish "queue-jumpers" trying to avoid going through the correct immigration procedures.

In Australia these techniques have been used to make refugees look as bad as possible. In 2001 it was claimed refugees on a sinking fishing boat (below left) threw children overboard to force the navy to rescue them and take them to Australia. These claims were quickly proven false.

When the container ship *Tampa* (below right) rescued hundreds of refugees from a sinking ship, armed SAS troops stopped them landing in Australia and all media reporting was tightly controlled to avoid sympathy developing for the asylum seekers.

Transfer is the tactic of linking something or somebody with a person or idea that already carries respect and authority, in order for those virtues to rub off and make them or it acceptable. Today, anyone closely linked with, say, a charity or other worthy cause is likely to receive some of the respect given to it. This transfer can of course work negatively and tarnish a person or idea by association. In the USA today, the accusation of being a "liberal" has a negative transfer effect, just as being called a "communist" did during the 1950s, as both are considered outside the mainstream of US politics.

Testimonial refers to receiving the personal endorsement of a well-liked person for a candidate or idea, in order for those who like that person to look more favourably on that candidate or idea. To say that you have Nelson Mandela's personal backing might well convince people to support you. This can also work negatively: if you have the prime minister's support, and he or she is very unpopular, your opponent will use that testimonial against you.

Plain folk: Try to convince an audience that a speaker is good and has good ideas because he or she is "of the people" or the "plain folks" of the world. There is often a natural distrust of government and authority, of "them". Identifying someone or something as being one of "us" will often help. But such appeals can be dangerous: Hitler was always described as a "man of the people", and Nazi propaganda praised him for his love of simple food and quiet living, even at the same time as they portrayed him as a superman who had come to return Germany to greatness.

Card stacking is the practice of carefully selecting and using relevant information regardless of whether it is true or false to present the best possible case for an idea or a person. Also known as "selective information", this too can be done negatively against an idea or person.

Bandwagon: Everyone likes to be on the winning side or part of a successful campaign. If you can create a campaign with the theme that "everyone is doing it", and that if you do not jump on the bandwagon you will be left behind, most people will be powerless to resist your cause. Most modern political campaigns use this technique, portraying a win-win situation of a win for their party being a win for you as well.

Man of the people?

One of the most successful attempts at portraying a national leader as one of the people was the Nazi propaganda about Adolf Hitler.

He was often described as a "man of the people", wearing ordinary clothes when not in military uniform, sporting no medals other than his Iron Cross, awarded for bravery during World War I, eating plain and simple food, and leading a quiet, secluded life.

Nazi propagandists consistently depicted him as an ordinary man, but one who could restore the self-respect of all Germans.

All clear? Now that you are armed with these seven tools of propaganda, you should be able to construct your own propaganda campaign and be able to see right through anyone else's. Next time you watch a film or an advert, read a book or newspaper, listen to a speech or a message from a political party, you will be able to work out just how much is propaganda, and how that propaganda works.

acronym
Pronounceable word made up of a series of initial letters or parts of words

agenda
List of items to be attended to

agitator
Person who promotes a cause through political or other action

agitprop
Agitational-Propaganda Section of the Central Committee of the Communist Party of the USSR; today, any promotion in the art of propaganda material

anti-Semitism
Racial hostility to Jews, expressed through discrimination and persecution of Jewish people

blockade
Military obstruction of a nation's access by land, sea, or air, preventing supplies or people reaching that nation

brainwashing
Form of propaganda in which a person is co-erced to believe what the enemy wishes

capitalism
Economic system based on the private ownership of industry, finance, and property, and where the state plays a minor role in the operation of the economic market

Chartists
Mass movement pressing for democratic rights, which flourished in Britain from 1838 to 1850; among its demands were universal adult male suffrage, secret voting, and annual parliaments

civilian
Citizen outside the military

Civil War, American
War of 1861–1865 between the northern Union states of the USA and the 11 southern states of the breakaway Confederacy over the issue of slavery, which the Confederate States wanted to continue; the war was intensely bitter, with more than 600,000 deaths; it ended with a northern victory and the emancipation of the slaves

Cold War
The war of words, ideas, and propaganda between the Western world and the Communist countries, which lasted from *c*.1945 to 1991

colonialism
Policy and practice of a nation in extending its control over other, usually weaker, nations or peoples

Crimean War
War between Britain, France, Sardinia, and the Ottoman Empire (Turkey) against Russia from 1853 to 1856, initially caused by disputes in Palestine about access to the holy Christian sites but actually aimed at restricting Russian access to the Mediterranean and the Middle East

communism
Belief in a society without different social classes in which everyone is equal, where all property is owned by the people, and where the state directs the economy and every aspect of daily life

conscript
Person who is enrolled for compulsory military service

counterpropaganda
Propaganda campaign mounted in opposition to another campaign and designed to neutralize or smother it

coup or coup d'état
Forcible seizure of power

democracy
Government by the people or their elected representatives, often forming opposing political parties

disinformation
Incorrect information issued with the express purpose of misleading people

electorate
Adult citizens eligible to vote in an election

fascist
Person who hold strong, right-wing, nationalist views, often of an anti-Semitic, anti-communist nature; fascists believe in the authority of the state over the individual

franchise
The right to vote

free trade
Trade between countries without any tariffs or duties between them

fundamentalism
Religious movements that favour strict interpretation of holy scriptures such as the Koran and the Bible

ideology
A body of coherent political beliefs and ideas

imperialist
Person who believes in the strength and importance of empire

manipulate
Handle or use someone or something with great skill in a process or action

market economy
Economy run on capitalist lines in which there is minimal intervention or control by the government

multinational
Operating in several countries

mutiny
Open rebellion by soldiers or seamen against their officers, usually punishable by death

Nazi Party
National Socialist Party, an extreme political party led by Adolf Hitler that ran Germany from 1933 to 1945.

neutral
Nation that refuses to take part in a war and does not fight

newsreel
Short film with a commentary presenting current events

patriotism
Love of one's country and concern for its defence

personality cult
Political movement of a set of beliefs based on the idolization of a single leader

propaganda, black
Propaganda where the source is hidden and the information largely false

propaganda, grey
Propaganda where the source might or might not be identified and the information might or might not be true

propaganda, white
Propaganda where the source is clear and the information accurate

psychology
Scientific study of all forms of human and animal behaviour, sometimes concerned with the methods through which such behaviour can be modified or controlled

subversive
Person who seeks to undermine or overthrow a government

superpower
Country with vast economic and military power. The USA is the only remaining superpower.

totalitarian state
Nation such as Nazi Germany or the communist Soviet Union where the state controls every aspect of society and regulates human behaviour

total war
War involving the entire civilian and military populations, fought using every human, social, industrial, psychological, and military weapon available

unconditional surrender
Surrender of a country without any conditions or limitations

United Nations
World organization set up in 1945 to work for peace and co-operation in the world

USSR
Union of the Soviet Socialist Republics, or the Soviet Union, which existed from 1922 to 1991; commonly known as Russia

Books

Bentley, Roy et al., *British Politics in Focus* (Causeway, 2004)

Clark, Toby, *Art and Propaganda in the Twentieth Century: The Political Image in the Age of Mass Culture* (Everyman, 1997)

Jowett, Gareth S., and O'Donnell, Victoria, *Propaganda and Persuasion* (3rd edn, Sage, 1999)

Parker, Steve, *1940s and 50s: The Power of Propaganda* (Heinemann Library, 2003)

Taylor, Philip M., *Munitions of the Mind: A History of Propaganda from the Ancient World to the Present Day* (Manchester University Press, 1995)

Websites

www.bbc.co.uk/history/war/wwtwo/nazi_propaganda_gallery_06.shtml – History of Nazi propaganda

www.propagandacritic.com
Devoted to critical analyses of propaganda, following in the footsteps of the IPA

www.ww1-propaganda-cards.com
Propaganda postcards of World War I

www.calvin.edu/academic/cas/gpa
German propaganda archive, Nazi and East Germany

www.sourcewatch.org/wiki.phtml?title=Disinfopedia
Wide range of information on propaganda in the world today

www.thematzats.com/propaganda/intro.htm
Various exercises and studies of propaganda

www.archives.gov/exhibit_hall/powers_of_persuasion/
powers_of_persuasion_home.html
Propaganda art in the US National Archives

Titles in the *Influence and Persuasion* series include:

Hardback 0431098328

Hardback 0431098336

Hardback 0431098344

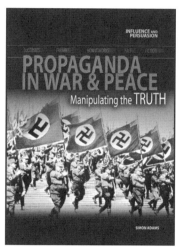

Hardback 0431098360

Hardback 0431098352

Find out about the other titles in this series on our website www.heinemann.co.uk/library